# SHELLY ANN FRASER PRYCE

# I AM A PROMISE

WITH **ASHLEY ROUSSEAU**
ILLUSTRATED BY **RACHEL MOSS**

*For Zyon, with love.*
—Shelly Ann Fraser Pryce

*For Miles & Joe, always.*
—Ashley Rousseau

Published by Akashic Books
Words ©2020 Shelly Ann Fraser Pryce & Ashley Rousseau
Illustrations ©2020 Rachel Moss

ISBN: 978-1-61775-764-8
Library of Congress Control Number: 2019935274
Second printing
Printed in China

Black Sheep/Akashic Books
Brooklyn, New York
Instagram: @AkashicBooks
Twitter: @AkashicBooks
Facebook: AkashicBooks
E-mail: info@akashicbooks.com
Website: www.akashicbooks.com

Hi there!

My hope is that you will enjoy reading this book. Coming from humble beginnings, I was blessed to have a family that loved and supported me, a nurturing environment which included my school, and coaches who encouraged and guided me along the way.

More importantly, my greatest gifts have been my faith and perseverance, as well as my trust in God and belief in my personal ability to overcome the challenges that life would send my way.

Both as an athlete and as a mother to Zyon, I have made a promise to myself to be the best I can be. It is my sincere hope that, no matter who you are or where you're from, you will also be inspired to make a promise to never give up on yourself, and to always do your very best.

*Fraser*

Shelly Ann Fraser Pryce

When I was a little girl, I dreamed of winning great races, but I was just a teeny-tiny thing in this wide, wondrous world.

As tiny as I was, I was also very fast and I loved to run, so . . .

I ran to school.

I ran to the shop.

I ran like a rocket.

I ran to be free.

I ran everywhere,
because that was me.

One day, my grandmother saw me running and she called me over: "Child, do you know that you are a promise?" I looked at her with wide eyes and asked, "What kind of promise, Granny?"

I was very confused. How could *I* be a promise? A promise is for ice cream on a Sunday. A promise is to keep your friend's secrets. How can a person be a promise?

But Granny just smiled and answered: "Don't worry, child, one day you will see."

As I grew older and entered big school, I kept running and training hard because that's what I loved to do, but now . . .

I ran faster than the other girls in races.
I ran faster than *everyone* in races.
I ran like a rocket.
I ran to be free.
I ran without fear, because that was me.

As the years went by, things were not always easy for my family. There were times when we struggled to pay the bills. There were times when we went to bed hungry. My mother often wondered how she would manage to take care of us all.

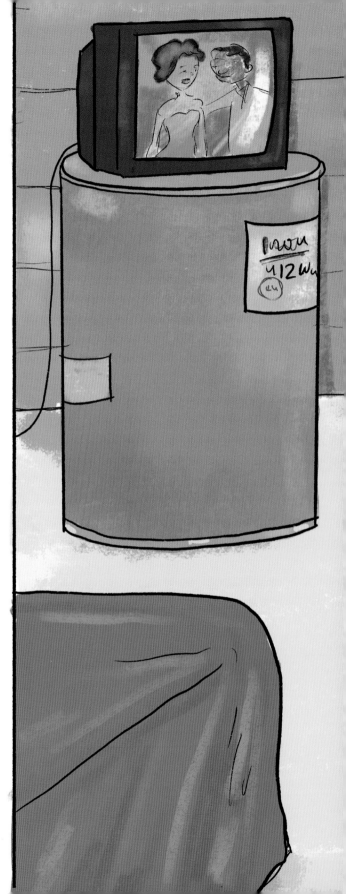

Thankfully, we met people along the way who said to me, "Young lady, you have great promise. We believe in you. We will help you."

I was glad for the help but still I wondered, *What is this promise that they say I have?* And, *Why me?*

Soon, an amazing thing happened. I ran so fast that I was chosen to run in the Olympics for my country, in a land far away. The stadium was filled with people from all over the world. The lights were bright. The cheering was very loud.

My heart beat fast. I was so nervous, but my coach said to me, "You represent the promise of our country. Go and show the world what this promise is."

I strode over to the blocks. I readied myself for the start. I thought of all my family and friends who had said that I was a promise. It was then that I knew:

I was a promise to my country and to all who have supported me. A promise to myself and to all those who have loved me. A promise to always be the best I can be.

The race began.

I ran for my country.
I ran for my friends and family.
I ran like a rocket.
I ran to be free.
But most important of all, I ran my best
because that was my promise to *me*.

# FAST FACTS:
## SHELLY ANN FRASER PRYCE

Born on December 27, 1986, Shelly Ann is a six-time Olympic medal winner.

## MEDAL RECORD

### OLYMPIC GAMES
Beijing 2008, London 2012, and Rio 2016

- 2 gold medals (100m)
- 3 silver medals (200m, 4x100m, 4x100m)
- 1 bronze medal (100m)

### WORLD CHAMPIONSHIPS
Osaka 2007, Berlin 2009, Daegu 2011, Moscow 2013, and Beijing 2015

- 8 gold medals (60m, 100m, 100m, 100m, 200m, 4x100m, 4x100m, 4x100m)
- 2 silver medals (4x100m)

# 10 THINGS TO KNOW ABOUT SHELLY ANN!

1. She is very spiritual and an active member of her Penwood Christ Church.
2. She rules under the sign of Capricorn and is extremely shy.
3. She would have pursued a career that involves working with children had she not become a professional athlete.
4. She loves bright colors, particularly pink and yellow.
5. She is the eldest of three children, with two younger brothers.
6. She is very enterprising, like her mother.
7. She has been a Goodwill Ambassador for UNICEF Jamaica since 2010.
8. She wants to pursue her master's degree in applied psychology when she retires from athletics.
9. She completed a degree in child and adolescent psychology prior to the 2012 London Olympics.
10. She married Jason Pryce in 2011, and gave birth to their son, Zyon Pryce, in 2017.

# ATHLETIC ACHIEVEMENTS

Shelly Ann was the fastest woman in the world in 2012, when she ran the 100m in 10.70 seconds.

In 2013, Shelly Ann was given the highest award in track-and-field athletics by being named the IAAF World Female Athlete of the Year after becoming the first woman in history to be a triple World Sprint champion, winning the 100m, 200m, and 4x100m at the World Championships in Athletics.

In 2014, Shelly Ann won the 60m gold at the World Indoor Championships, thereby becoming the first woman in history from any nation to simultaneously be the reigning world champion in the 60m, 100m, 200m, 4x100m, and Olympic champion in the 100m.

In August 2015, Shelly Ann became the first female in history to win three 100m gold medals in the World Championships.

Shelly Ann was awarded Jamaica's Sports Performance of the Year in 2008 and Sports Woman of the Year in 2012, 2013, and 2015. She was the 2012 IAAF Diamond League Champion in the 100m.

**SHELLY ANN FRASER PRYCE** is a six-time Olympic medal winner and holds several prestigious national and world athletic titles. In 2008, she received the prime minister's Youth Award for Excellence in Sport, and in 2014 was conferred with the title Ambassador at Large for Jamaica. In recognizing her contribution to sport and the country as a whole, the government of Jamaica appointed Shelly Ann an Officer of the Order of Distinction in 2008, and unveiled a statue of her at the National Stadium in 2018. In 2016, both the University of the West Indies and the University of Technology, Jamaica, presented Shelly Ann with the honorary degree of Doctor of Laws. A UNICEF Goodwill Ambassador, she is also the founder of the Pocket Rocket Foundation, which assists promising high school athletes; and the owner of Shelly's Café, and a hair salon, Lady Shelly Beauty. Shelly Ann is married to Jason Pryce and they have a son, Zyon, who was born in August 2017. She is endorsed by Nike, GraceKennedy, and Digicel Jamaica.

Photo by Mustafa Yalcin/Anadolu Agency/Getty Images